A painter, poet and engraver, William Blake (1757–1827) was born in London. *Poetical Sketches*, his first volume of poetry, was published in 1783 and was followed by several of his best-known works: *Songs of Innocence* (1789), *The Book of Thel* (1789), *The Marriage of Heaven and Hell* (1790–3), *Songs of Experience* (1794) and *Jerusalem* (1804–20).

James Fenton was born in Lincoln in 1949 and educated at Magdalen College, Oxford. He has worked as political journalist, drama critic, book reviewer, foreign correspondent and columnist. He was Oxford Professor of Poetry from 1994 to 1999. Lectures are collected in *The Strengh of Poetry* and his art criticism in *Leonardo's Nephew*. He edited *The New Faber Book of Love Poems* (2006), and his *Selected Poems* was published in 2006. He is a recipient of the Queen's Gold Medal for Poetry.

# WILLIAM BLAKE

## Poems selected by JAMES FENTON

*faber and faber*

First published in 2010
by Faber and Faber Limited
Bloomsbury House, 74–77 Great Russell Street
London WC1B 3DA

Typeset by RefineCatch Ltd, Bungay, Suffolk
Printed in England by CPI BookMarque, Croydon

A CIP record for this book
is available from the British Library

ISBN 978–0–571–23603–9

10 9 8 7 6 5 4 3 2 1

# Contents

THE MARRIAGE OF HEAVEN AND HELL (?1790–3)

# Introduction

'Greatness,' said T. S. Eliot, 'is not a state that poets really seek; greatness is a matter, so far as we are concerned, of chance, of what happens afterwards when we are dead; and that depends upon a great many things outside of ourselves.' It is certainly true of William Blake that, whatever his contemporaries thought of him as an artist and poet, they would not have expected him to be ranked as one of the greatest writers of his era.

Few of them would have been in a position to form a judgement on the matter anyway, though some of his poems were circulated by enthusiasts. These short lyrics were admired, but they were thought to be the work of a madman. Walter Savage Landor was 'strangely fascinated' by them, and told his future biographer that 'Blake had been Wordsworth's proto-type', and that he 'wished they could have divided his madness between them; for that some accession of it in the one case, and something of a diminution of it in the other, would have greatly improved both.' Charles Lamb used to call Blake a 'mad Wordsworth', while Wordsworth himself remarked of Blake: 'There is no doubt that this man is mad, but there is something in this madness which I enjoy more than the Sense of W: Sc: [Walter Scott] or Lord B.'

Some time in 1807, Wordsworth and his sister Dorothy copied out 'Holy Thursday', 'Laughing Song', 'The Tyger' and the song 'I Love the Jocund Dance' into a commonplace book. Coleridge, in 1818, returning a copy of Blake's *Songs of Innocence and Experience*, provided his correspondent with a key to his reactions to individual poems. The letter 'I' meant 'It gave me great pleasure,' while 'Θ' meant 'It gave me pleasure in the highest degree.' 'The Divine Image' and 'Night' were both top-scorers, while 'The Little Black Boy' was rated 'Θ: yea Θ + Θ!'

You can see, from this kind of evidence, that Blake as a poet was, in his day, only inches away from the highest sort of recog-nition. But those were significant inches, and we cannot even be sure that it was the artist-poet that John Clare was referring to when he wrote: 'Blake was brave by instinct & honest by choice.' But it makes a nice tribute.

In 1811, Henry Crabb Robinson, the diarist and early essayist on Blake, read some of the poems to Hazlitt, who was 'much struck with them & expressed himself with his usual strength & singularity. "They are beautiful," he said, "& only too deep for the vulgar; he has no sense of the ludicrous & as to God a worm crawling in a privy is as worthy an object as any other, all being to him indifferent. So to Blake the Chimney Sweeper &c. He is ruined by vain struggles to get rid of what presses on his brain – he attempts impossibles –"' To which Crabb Robinson replied that Blake was 'like a man who lifts a burthen too heavy for him; he bears it an instant, then it falls on and crushes him'.

The full recognition of Blake's genius began during the last decade of his life (1757–1827), with the adulation of the 'Ancients' – artists such as Samuel Palmer, Edward Calvert, John Linnell and George Richmond. But the piety of this circle brought with it a very serious drawback: it was one of Blake's admirers, Frederick Tatham, who appears to have burnt a large number of Blake's manuscripts. He was a zealous member of a Christian sect called the Irvingites. Tatham is said to have been 'instigated to it by some very influential members of the Sect on the ground that Blake was inspired; but from quite the wrong quarter – by Satan himself – and was to be cast out as an "unclean spirit"'.

Quite what was destroyed is impossible to know: according to one source, 'volumes of verse, amounting, it is said, to nearly an hundred, prepared for the press'. Was Blake exaggerating when he told Crabb Robinson that he had 'written more than Voltaire or Rousseau – Six or Seven Epic poems as long as Homer and 20 tragedies as long as Macbeth'? Well, *Macbeth* is actually one of the shorter tragedies, but this emphasis on length is a little ominous: it is hard to pine, exactly, for the loss of those epic poems. What does not bear contemplating is the putative loss of things not mentioned in this list: notebooks, lyric poems, epigrams.

If what was destroyed was believed to be inspired by Satan, we may imagine that it included works that were found to be anti-monarchical, heretical and sexually outrageous. Blake seems to have intended to write 'The Bible of Hell', for he drafted a title page for it, subtitled 'in Nocturnal Visions collected Vol. I Lambeth'. And another, or perhaps the same, project: 'For Children the Gates of Hell'. Crabb Robinson says that Blake 'shewed me his Version (for so it may be called) of Genesis – "as understood by a Christian Visionary" in which in a style resembling the Bible – The spirit is given. He read a passage at random. It was striking.' But G. E. Bentley, who sets out all the evidence for Lost Works in his edition of Blake's writings, concludes that nothing resembling a Version of Genesis is known.

Blake himself, in the year before his death, told Crabb Robinson:

> 'I have been tempted to burn my MSS but my wife wont let me.' 'She is right,' said I – 'You have written these, not from yourself but by a higher order. The MSS. are theirs not your property – You cannot tell what purpose they may answer; unforeseen to you.' He liked this and said he would not destroy them . . .

It is ironic that here we find the reason for preserving the writings to be the same as the reason for destroying them: they were inspired by a higher order, whether Satanic or otherwise.

It is exasperating to read of Dante Gabriel Rossetti, one of the key Victorian advocates of Blake's work, throwing into his waste-basket some sheets containing 'bad' verses, 'from which Swinburne rescued a few fragments not quite so worthless as the rest'. And Anne Gilchrist, the widow of Blake's pioneering biographer, burnt 'a prose narrative of a domestic, and also fantastic, sort, clearly intended by its author to count as humouristic or funny, and somewhat in the Shandean vein.'

No doubt this destroyed work was something like the nonsensical 'An Island in the Moon', most of whose satire and purpose is obscure to us. The fact that I have not included 'An Island' in this selection does not mean it does not interest me. *Vala or The Four Zoas*, on the other hand (for whose first publication Yeats was partially responsible), is more than I can face. Of course I am glad it escaped the bonfire. But this is not the Blake who so effortlessly commands our highest respect, prompting comparisons, in Eliot's essay in *The Sacred Wood*, with Homer, Aeschylus, Dante and Villon.

What the source of that greatness is, Eliot answers in a striking way:

> It is merely a peculiar honesty, which, in a world too frightened to be honest, is peculiarly terrifying. It is an honesty against which the world conspires, because it is unpleasant. Blake's poetry has the unpleasantness of great poetry. Nothing that can be called morbid or abnormal or perverse, none of the things which exemplify the sickness of an epoch or a fashion, have this quality; only those things which, by some extraordinary labour of simplification, exhibit the essential sickness or strength of the human soul.

It is not hard to think of lines that exemplify this unpleasantness. The celebrated conclusion of 'The Poison Tree' for instance:

> In the morning glad I see
> My foe outstretched beneath the tree.

The use of the word 'glad' in such a context has a terrific force, as in Drayton:

> Since there's no help, come let us kiss and part,
> Nay, I have done: you get no more of me,
> And I am glad, yea glad with all my heart,
> That thus so cleanly I myself can free . . .

But the whole psychological argument of 'A Poison Tree' was in its time completely original, and displays – if Blake is to be admired for his 'peculiar honesty' – an extraordinary insight into deceit.

> There is a Smile of Love
> And there is a Smile of Deceit
> And there is a Smile of Smiles
> In which these two Smiles meet . . .

This from the 'The Smile', the poem from which Yeats borrowed, and adapted, the phrase 'the Hearts deep Core' which turns up at the end of 'The Lake Isle of Innisfree' – Yeats being as much in debt to Blake as Auden was.

> The look of love alarms
> Because tis filld with fire
> But the look of soft deceit
> Shall Win the lovers hire.

'Soft deceit' turns up again as a manifestation of beauty, and there is a strong sense of deceit hovering around the following transactions:

> I asked a thief to steal me a peach.
> He turned up his eyes.
> I askd a lithe lady to lie her down.
> Holy & meek she cries.
>
> As soon as I went
> An angel came.
> He winkd at the thief
> And smild at the dame
>
> And without one word said
> Had a peach from the tree
> And still as a maid
> Enjoy'd the lady.

What could the moral of this poem possibly be, other than 'Don't ask, if you don't want to receive a hypocritical refusal'? But what sort of angel are we talking about, who goes around stealing peaches and making love to holy-seeming ladies? This is one of the many mysteries of Blake, and a source of his great attractiveness to modern taste.

There is religion here, but there is no orthodoxy. Everything depends on what seems to Blake to be true. There is a reverence for Christ, matched by a hatred for what the church has done in his name. The little boy in the second of the two poems called 'A Little Boy Lost' is boldly heterodox, not to say heretical, when he declares that:

Nought loves another as itself
Nor venerates another so.
Nor is it possible to Thought
A greater than itself to know:

And Father, how can I love you,
Or any of my brothers more?
I love you as the little bird
That picks the crumbs around the door.

He is like Cordelia when she, with catastrophic consequences, refuses to flatter Lear. In a sense he is more provocative than Cordelia. She tells Lear she loves him 'According to my bond; no more, no less.' And she expounds the meaning of this. 'Good my Lord,' she explains,

You have begot me, bred me, lov'd me: I
Return those duties back as are right fit,
Obey you, love you, and most honour you.

Cordelia's love is conventional. But the little boy questions both the commandment to love the Lord thy God, but also the possibility of Thought apprehending something larger than itself. For this answer the little boy is taken by the priest to a holy place, where he is burned alive. The last line of the poem is missing a question mark in Blake's engraved version: 'Are such things done on Albions shore.' But many a priest might have objected that, no, they are not. Children were not burnt at the stake for heterodoxy. Indeed, nobody was being burnt at the stake for heresy in Britain at the time Blake wrote.* And yet Blake's forcefulness convinces us that the poem is in some sense true. So we must look for the sense in which it *is* true.

The sense would be something along these lines: that the cruelty of Christian doctrine as forced upon a child's innocent spiritual nature amounts to a kind of murder. The threat of hell fire is like a sort of burning at the stake. Blake may have been saying this, but he was still a Christian himself, and in his *Songs of Innocence*, especially, he was working within a tradition of religious versification for children which goes back to Bunyan and Isaac Watts. Indeed, among the earliest printed references to Blake's poetry we find an unflattering comparison with Watts. If Watts, says a writer in the *Monthly Review* (October 1806), 'seldom rose above the level of a mere versifier, in what class must we place Mr. Blake, who is certainly very inferior to Watts?'

It is the misfortune of Watts (1674–1748) to be remembered through Lewis Carroll's parodies of his moralising children's poems in *Alice in Wonderland*. He was immensely successful as a hymnographer, and an American survey published in 1891 estimated that two-fifths of the hymns in 750 hymn-books were those of Watts. Of the 697 hymns he wrote, 191 were then still in use in Calvinist churches. They include 'Come Let Us Join Our Cheerful Songs', 'Give me the Wings of Faith to Rise', 'Jesus Shall Reign Where'er the Sun', 'There Is a Land of Pure Delight' and 'When I Survey the Wondrous Cross'.

As with much popular literature, the texts of these hymns were continually revised and updated, to make them conform to later taste. This means that, even if we are aware of Watts's

---

* Women were burnt at the stake for murdering their husbands or for counterfeiting coinage (both crimes seen as a form of treason) until 1789. In 1741, in New York, thirteen African men were burnt at the stake for rebellious conspiracy, and the practice of burning blacks at the stake, often on accusation of murder or rape, continued in America as a form of lynching into the mid-twentieth century.

hymns, we may know them in inferior versions, with omissions and the kind of improvements we would not tolerate in poetic texts. The last two verses of 'When I Survey' give us a sense of Watts at his best:

His dying Crimson like a Robe
Spreads o're his Body on the Tree,
Then I am dead to all the Globe,
And all the Globe is dead to me.

Were the whole Realm of Nature mine,
That were a Present far to small;
Love so amazing, so divine
Demands my Soul, my Life, my All.

The first of these verses is often omitted in church, while in the second the word 'Present' is usually changed to 'Offering'. (A final verse, not by Watts, was added in *Hymns Ancient and Modern*.) Such rewriting has been traditionally accepted, because the hymn is seen as belonging to the church, not to its author. If someone were to assert that Watts was our Luther, that claim would be hard to dismiss. 'We might almost say,' as an American source puts it, 'that before Watts, English churches sang Psalms. After Watts, they sang Hymns.'

Lewis Carroll does not parody the hymns – that would have been unthinkable. What he delights in sinking is the poetry for children. Here is Watts in his *Divine Songs for Children* (1715, and still going strong in the nursery 150 years later):

How doth the little busy bee
    Improve each shining hour,
And gather honey all the day
    From every open flower!

How skilfully she builds the cell!
    How neat she spreads the wax!
And labours hard to store it well
    With the sweet food she makes.

In words of labour or of skill,
  I would be busy too;
For Satan finds some mischief still
  For idle hands to do.

In books, or works, or healthful play,
  Let my first years be passed,
That I may give for every day
  Some good account at last.

Blake perhaps alludes to this poem when he places among his
Proverbs of Hell: 'The busy bee has no time for sorrow.' And
here is Carroll, setting up a moment in which Alice, misremem-
bering Watts, believes, because she is getting the words wrong,
that she must be ignorant Mabel after all:

How doth the little crocodile
  Improve his shining tail,
And pour the waters of the Nile
  On every golden scale!

How cheerfully he seems to grin,
  How neatly spreads his claws,
And welcomes little fishes in,
  With gently smiling jaws.

The poem stops at this point with Alice's 'I'm sure those are not
the right words', before the moral can be drawn – the joke being
that there is no way Alice should be emulating a crocodile.
  Here again is the opening of another Watts poem:

'Tis the voice of the sluggard; I heard him complain,
'You have wak'd me too soon, I must slumber again.'
As the door on its hinges, so he on his bed,
Turns his sides and his shoulders and his heavy head.

This in Carroll's hands becomes:

'Tis the voice of the Lobster: I heard him declare
'You have baked me too brown, I must sugar my hair.'

As a duck with its eyelids, so he with his nose
Trims his belt and his buttons and turns out his toes.

And so on.

Where Carroll takes delight in sinking Watts entirely, by turning him into pure nonsense, Blake has been thought to be answering him back. Here is an illustration of the way Bunyan, Watts and Blake were working in the same tradition of children's poetry, moralising from the works of nature. It has been noted that each has a poems about the ant, or 'pismire', taking off from the Book of Proverbs, chapter 6, verse 6: 'Go to the ant, thou sluggard; consider her ways and be wise.' Here is Bunyan 'Upon the Pismire':

Must we unto the Pis-mire go to School,
To learn of her, in Summer to provide
For Winter next ensuing; Man's a Fool,
Or silly Ants would not be made his Guide.
But Sluggard, is it not a shame for thee,
To be out-done by Pis-mires? Prethee hear:
Their works (too) will thy Condemnation bee,
When at the Judgment seat thou shalt appear.
But since thy God doth bid thee to her go,
Obey, her ways consider, and be wise.
The Piss-ants tell thee will what thou must do,
And set the way to Life before thine eyes.

No evidence here that Bunyan had looked closely at, or thought very hard about, the ant. Indeed the starting-point of the lesson is an acknowledged reluctance to take a biblical lesson to heart. And Bunyan is a rudimentary naturalist:

The Frog by Nature is both damp and cold,
Her Mouth is large, her Belly much will hold:
She sits somewhat ascending, loves to be
Croaking in Gardens, tho unpleasantly.

There is not much joy in this description, whose purpose is to set the frog up as the emblem of the ecclesiastical hypocrite.

Watts, though by aptitude not a nature poet, was a creature of the Enlightenment who had clearly looked through a microscope and been amazed by what he had seen. He had looked, and he seems to have recognised that if he went on looking too hard his whole spiritual system would be in danger of crashing to the ground. At least that is what I take this passage to suggest.

> An exquisite World of Wonders is complicated even in the Body of every little Insect, an Ant, a Gnat, a Mite, that is scarce visible to the naked Eye. Admirable Engines! which a whole Academy of Philosophers could never contrive, which the Nation of Poets hath neither Art nor Colours to describe; nor has the World of Mechanics Skill enough to frame the plainest, or coarsest of them. Their Nurves, their Muscles, and the minute Atoms which compose the Fluids fit to run in the little Channels of their Veins, escape the Notice of the most sagacious Mathematician, with all his Aid of Glasses. The active Powers and Curiosity of Human Nature are limited in their Pursuit, and must be content to lie down in Ignorance. – *Hitherto shall ye go and no further.*

Watts has an admirable short essay or meditation upon the destruction of a hornets' nest, from which we can see that, had circumstances been a little different, he might well have become a naturalist – but if he had done so, he would, just like the clergy of the nineteenth century, have had to ask those awkward questions, and not be 'content to lie down in ignorance'. Sooner or later there would have been a crisis.

Blake, by contrast, saw the crisis in the here and now, in the world as proposed by Newton and the rationalists:

> Mock on Mock on Voltaire Rousseau
> Mock on Mock on tis all in vain
> You throw the sand against the wind
> And the wind blows it back again
>
> And every sand becomes a Gem
> Reflected in the beams divine

Blown back they blind the mocking Eye
But still in Israel's paths they shine

The Atoms of Democritus
And Newtons Particles of light
Are sand upon the Red sea shore
Where Israels tents do shine so bright

That is, the scientific view of the world blinds its adherents to revelation. Blake was by no means indifferent to nature. 'The Tyger' after all presents an awestruck vision of the natural world. But it is the vision that counts. Blake apparently knew the illustrations to Robert Hook's *Micrographia*, which influence the conception of his extraordinary drawing of 'The Ghost of a Flea'. But the anthropomorphic conception of this ghost belongs to Blake's vision alone.

Watts's song 'The Ant or Emmet' is a wordy piece of moralising, no better or worse than Bunyan's:

These emmets, how little they are in our eyes!
We tread them to dust, and a troop of them dies,
    Without our regard or concern:
Yet as wise as we are, if we went to their school,
There's many a sluggard and many a fool,
    Some lessons of wisdom might learn.

And so on. Blake's 'A Dream' takes us to a quite different level.

Once a dream did weave a shade,
O'er my Angel-guarded bed,
That an Emmet lost it's way
Where on grass methought I lay.

Troubled wilderd and forlorn
Dark benighted travel-worn,
Over many a tangled spray
All heart-broke I heard her say.

O my children! Do they cry
Do they hear their father sigh.

Now they look abroad to see,
Now return and weep for me.

Pitying I drop'd a tear:
But I saw a glow-worm near:
Who replied. What wailing wight
Calls the watchman of the night.

I am set to light the ground,
While the beetle goes his round:
Follow now the beetles hum,
Little wanderer hie thee home.

Blake could never have seen this through a microscope or observed it in the natural world, and the biblical text has been left far behind: we are here in an imaginary kingdom in which the animals feel sympathy for each other's sufferings, and help each other out, just as the god of the next poem, 'On Anothers Sorrow', is a fellow-suffering, not a vengeful god.

He doth give his joy to all.
He becomes an infant small.
He becomes a man of woe
He doth feel the sorrow too.

Blake's point of departure, in the *Songs of Innocence*, might indeed be viewed as a criticism of Watts and his contemporaries for the cruelty of their doctrine and particularly their cruelty towards children. Here is Watts, talking to infants:

Cross Words and angry Names require
    To be chastiz'd at School;
And he's in danger of Hell-fire,
    That calls his Brother, Fool.

But Lips that dare be so prophane
    To mock and jeer and scoff
At Holy Things or Holy Men,
    The Lord shall cut them off.

When Children in their wanton Play
    Serv'd old *Elisha* so,
And bid the Prophet go his way,
    '*Go up, thou Bald-head, go,*'

God quickly stopt their wicked Breath,
    And sent too raging Bears,
That tore them Limb from Limb to Death
    With Blood and Groans and Tears.

The first of these stanzas is a versification of Matthew 5 : 22, the last two relate an incident from 2 Kings 2, but there is a crucial element of choice in this. Nobody obliged Watts to threaten children, in his poetry, in this way:

Have we not heard what dreadful Plagues
    Are threatened by the Lord
To him that breaks his Father's Law,
    Or mocks his Mother's Word?

What heavy Guilt upon his lies!
    How cursed is his name!
The Ravens shall peck out his Eyes,
    And Eagles eat the same.

One feels there must be other ways of teaching the lesson of the song, which is 'Obedience to Parents.'

Clearly Blake thought so too. Or rather, clearly Blake took a more nuanced view of parents and the obedience due to them, for while God (in the Song of Innocence and Experience) has the qualities of a loving father, actual fathers are not a great feature in Blake's poetry. Childhood here often seems like an orphaned state, or one against which the child must rebel:

Struggling in my fathers hands
Striving against my swaddling bands
Bound & weary I thought best
To sulk upon my mothers breast

In the longer manuscript version of 'Infant Sorrow' the father curses the son, and binds him in a myrtle shade. And the son stages a bloody rebellion.

The parents of the chimney sweeper are pious and neglectful:

A little black thing among the snow:
Crying weep, weep, in notes of woe!
Where are thy father & mother? say?
They are both gone to the church to pray.

This, and the ensuing stanzas, would have shocked Watts deeply. It pleased Coleridge, as his notation shows, 'in the lowest [degree]'.

No one had written anything remotely like this before. No one had thought to attack the Church and the monarchy and parenthood in a single short poem. No one had written a ballad as strange and powerful as 'The Mental Traveller', with its vision of life in reverse, the baby being born in joy (as opposed to the agony of childbirth) and immediately tormented by his nurse:

And if the Babe is born a Boy
He's given to a Woman Old
Who nails him down upon a rock
Catches his shrieks in cups of gold

No one had thought of composing a story in which, as one character grows older, another grows younger, let alone proposed this reverse process as a cyclical quality of human experience. It is indeed, as Eliot said, peculiarly terrifying.

Her fingers number every Nerve
Just as a Miser counts his gold
She lives upon his shrieks & cries
And she grows young as he grows old

Till he becomes a bleeding youth
And she becomes a Virgin bright
Then he rends up his Manacles
And binds her down for his delight

As Hazlitt said, Blake 'attempts impossibles'. But a century was to pass before there were readers who, like Eliot, Yeats and Auden, were ready to acknowledge the strangest successes of these attempts.

JAMES FENTON

# WILLIAM BLAKE

## Song

How sweet I roam'd from field to field,
  And tasted all the summer's pride,
'Till I the prince of love beheld,
  Who in the sunny beams did glide!

He shew'd me lilies for my hair,
  And blushing roses for my brow;
He led me through his gardens fair,
  Where all his golden pleasures grow.

With sweet May dews my wings were wet,
  And Phoebus fir'd my vocal rage;
He caught me in his silken net,
  And shut me in his golden cage.

He loves to sit and hear me sing,
  Then, laughing, sports and plays with me;
Then stretches out my golden wing,
  And mocks my loss of liberty.

# Song

I love the jocund dance,
    The softly-breathing song,
Where innocent eyes do glance,
    And where lisps the maiden's tongue.

I love the laughing vale,
    I love the echoing hill,
Where mirth does never fail,
    And the jolly swain laughs his fill.

I love the pleasant cot,
    I love the innocent bow'r.
Where white and brown is our lot,
    Or fruit in the mid-day hour.

I love the oaken seat,
    Beneath the oaken tree,
Where all the old villagers meet,
    And laugh our sports to see.

I love our neighbours all,
    But, Kitty, I better love thee;
And love them I ever shall;
    But thou art all to me.

## Introduction

Piping down the valleys wild
Piping songs of pleasant glee
On a cloud I saw a child.
And he laughing said to me.

Pipe a song about a Lamb;
So I piped with merry chear,
Piper pipe that song again –
So I piped, he wept to hear.

Drop thy pipe thy happy pipe
Sing thy songs of happy chear,
So I sung the same again
While he wept with joy to hear

Piper sit thee down and write
In a book that all may read –
So he vanish'd from my sight.
And I pluck'd a hollow reed.

And I made a rural pen,
And I stain'd the water clear,
And I wrote my happy songs
Every child may joy to hear

# The Shepherd

How sweet is the Shepherds sweet lot,
From the morn to the evening he strays:
He shall follow his sheep all the day
And his tongue shall be filled with praise.

For he hears the lambs innocent call.
And he hears the ewes tender reply.
He is watchful while they are in peace.
For they know when their Shepherd is nigh.

## The Ecchoing Green

The Sun does arise,
And make happy the skies.
The merry bells ring
To welcome the Spring.
The sky-lark and thrush,
The birds of the bush,
Sing louder around.
To the bells chearful sound.
While our sports shall be seen
On the Ecchoing Green.

Old John with white hair
Does laugh away care,
Sitting under the oak,
Among the old folk,
They laugh at our play,
And soon they all say.
Such such were the joys.
When we all girls & boys,
In our youth-time were seen,
On the Ecchoing Green.

Till the little ones weary
No more can be merry
The sun does descend.
And our sports have an end:
Round the laps of their mothers,
Many sisters and brothers,
Like birds in their nest,
Are ready for rest;
And sport no more seen,
On the darkening Green.

# The Lamb

    Little Lamb who made thee
    Dost thou know who made thee
Gave thee life & bid thee feed.
By the stream & o'er the mead;
Gave thee clothing of delight,
Softest clothing wooly bright;
Gave thee such a tender voice,
Making all the vales rejoice:
    Little Lamb who made thee
    Dost thou know who made thee

    Little Lamb I'll tell thee,
    Little Lamb I'll tell thee:
He is called by thy name,
For he calls himself a Lamb:
He is meek & he is mild,
He became a little child:
I a child & thou a lamb,
We are called by his name.
    Little Lamb God bless thee.
    Little Lamb God bless thee.

# The Little Black Boy

My mother bore me in the southern wild,
And I am black, but O! my soul is white;
White as an angel is the English child:
But I am black as if bereav'd of light.

My mother taught me underneath a tree
And sitting down before the heat of day,
She took me on her lap and kissed me,
And pointing to the east began to say.

Look on the rising sun: there God does live
And gives his light, and gives his heat away.
And flowers and trees and beasts and men receive
Comfort in morning joy in the noon day.

And we are put on earth a little space,
That we may learn to bear the beams of love,
And these black bodies and this sun-burnt face
Is but a cloud, and like a shady grove.

For when our souls have learn'd the heat to bear
The cloud will vanish we shall hear his voice.
Saying: come out from the grove my love & care,
And round my golden tent like lambs rejoice.

Thus did my mother say and kissed me,
And thus I say to little English boy.
When I from black and he from white cloud free,
And round the tent of God like lambs we joy:

Ill shade him from the heat till he can bear,
To lean in joy upon our fathers knee.
And then I'll stand and stroke his silver hair,
And be like him and he will then love me.

# The Blossom

Merry Merry Sparrow
Under leaves so green
A happy Blossom
Sees you swift as arrow
Seek your cradle narrow
Near my Bosom.

Pretty Pretty Robin
Under leaves so green
A happy Blossom
Hears you sobbing sobbing
Pretty Pretty Robin
Near my Bosom.

## The Chimney Sweeper

When my mother died I was very young,
And my father sold me while yet my tongue,
Could scarcely cry weep weep weep weep.
So your chimneys I sweep & in soot I sleep.

Theres little Tom Dacre, who cried when his head
That curl'd like a lambs back, was shav'd, so I said.
Hush Tom never mind it, for when your head's bare,
You know that the soot cannot spoil your white hair.

And so he was quiet, & that very night,
As Tom was a sleeping he had such a sight,
That thousands of sweepers Dick, Joe Ned & Jack
Were all of them lock'd up in coffins of black

And by came an Angel who had a bright key,
And he open'd the coffins & set them all free.
Then down a green plain leaping laughing they run
And wash in a river and shine in the Sun.

Then naked & white, all their bags left behind,
They rise upon clouds, and sport in the wind.
And the Angel told Tom if he'd be a good boy,
He'd have God for his father & never want joy.

And so Tom awoke and we rose in the dark
And got with our bags & our brushes to work.
Tho' the morning was cold, Tom was happy & warm,
So if all do their duty, they need not fear harm.

## The Little Boy Lost

Father, father, where are you going
O do not walk so fast.
Speak father, speak to your little boy
Or else I shall be lost,

The night was dark no father was there
The child was wet with dew.
The mire was deep, & the child did weep
And away the vapour flew.

# The Little Boy Found

The little boy lost in the lonely fen,
Led by the wand'ring light,
Began to cry, but God ever nigh,
Appeard like his father in white.

He kissed the child & by the hand led
And to his mother brought,
Who is sorrow pale, thro' the lonely dale
Her little boy weeping sought.

## Laughing Song

When the green woods laugh, with the voice of joy
And the dimpling stream runs laughing by,
When the air does laugh with our merry wit,
And the green hill laughs with the noise of it.

When the meadows laugh with lively green
And the grasshopper laughs in the merry scene,
When Mary and Susan and Emily,
With their sweet round mouths sing Ha, Ha, He.

When the painted birds laugh in the shade
Where our table with cherries and nuts is spread
Come live & be merry and join with me,
To sing the sweet chorus of Ha, Ha, He.

# A Cradle Song

Sweet dreams form a shade,
O'er my lovely infants head.
Sweet dreams of pleasant streams.
By happy silent moony beams.

Sweet sleep with soft down,
Weave thy brows an infant crown.
Sweet sleep Angel mild,
Hover o'er my happy child.

Sweet smiles in the night,
Hover over my delight.
Sweet smiles Mothers smiles
All the livelong night beguiles.

Sweet moans, dovelike sighs,
Chase not slumber from thy eyes.
Sweet moans, sweeter smiles.
All the dovelike moans beguiles.

Sleep sleep happy child.
All creation slept and smil'd.
Sleep sleep happy sleep.
While o'er thee thy mother weep

Sweet babe in thy face,
Holy image I can trace.
Sweet babe once like thee,
Thy maker lay and wept for me

Wept for me for thee for all.
When he was an infant small.
Thou his image ever see.
Heavenly face that smiles on thee.

Smiles on thee on me on all,
Who became an infant small,
Infant smiles are his own smiles.
Heaven & earth to peace beguiles.

# The Divine Image

To Mercy Pity Peace and Love,
All pray in their distress:
And to these virtues of delight
Return their thankfulness.

For Mercy Pity Peace and Love,
Is God our father dear:
And Mercy Pity Peace and Love,
Is Man his child and care.

For Mercy has a human heart
Pity, a human face:
And Love, the human form divine,
And Peace, the human dress.

Then every man of every clime,
That prays in his distress,
Prays to the human form divine
Love Mercy Pity Peace.

And all must love the human form,
In heathen, turk or jew.
Where Mercy, Love & Pity dwell
There God is dwelling too.

## Holy Thursday

Twas on a Holy Thursday their innocent faces clean
The children walking two & two in red & blue & green
Grey headed beadles walkd before with wands as white as snow
Till into the high dome of Pauls they like Thames waters flow

O what a multitude they seemd these flowers of London town
Seated in companies they sit with radiance all their own
The hum of multitudes was there but multitudes of lambs
Thousands of little boys & girls raising their innocent hands

Now like a mighty wind they raise to heaven the voice of song
Or like harmonious thunderings the seats of heaven among
Beneath them sit the aged men wise guardians of the poor
Then cherish pity, lest you drive an angel from your door

# Night

The sun descending in the west
The evening star does shine.
The birds are silent in their nest,
And I must seek for mine,
The moon like a flower,
In heavens high bower;
With silent delight,
Sits and smiles on the night.

Farewell green fields and happy groves,
Where flocks have took delight;
Where lambs have nibbled, silent moves
The feet of angels bright;
Unseen they pour blessing,
And joy without ceasing,
On each bud and blossom,
And each sleeping bosom.

They look in every thoughtless nest,
Where birds are coverd warm;
They visit caves of every beast,
To keep them all from harm;
If they see any weeping,
That should have been sleeping
They pour sleep on their head
And sit down by their bed.

When wolves and tygers howl for prey
They pitying stand and weep;
Seeking to drive their thirst away,
And keep them from the sheep.
But if they rush dreadful;
The angels most heedful,
Receive each mild spirit,
New worlds to inherit.

And there the lions ruddy eyes,
Shall flow with tears of gold:
And pitying the tender cries,
And walking round the fold:
Saying: wrath by his meekness
And by his health, sickness,
Is driven away,
From our immortal day.

And now beside thee bleating lamb,
I can lie down and sleep;
Or think on him who bore thy name,
Grase after thee and weep.
For wash'd in lifes river,
My bright mane for ever.
Shall shine like the gold.
As I guard o'er the fold.

# Spring

Sound the Flute!
Now it's mute.
Birds delight
Day and Night.
Nightingale
In the dale
Lark in Sky
Merrily
Merrily Merrily to welcome in the Year

Little Boy
Full of joy.
Little Girl
Sweet and small,
Cock does crow
So do you.
Merry voice
Infant noise
Merrily Merrily to welcome in the Year

Little Lamb
Here I am,
Come and lick
My white neck.
Let me pull
Your soft Wool.
Let me kiss
Your soft face.
Merrily Merrily we welcome in the Year

## Nurse's Song

When the voices of children are heard on the green
And laughing is heard on the hill,
My heart is at rest within my breast
And every thing else is still

Then come home my children, the sun is gone down
And the dews of night arise
Come come leave off play, and let us away
Till the morning appears in the skies

No no let us play, for it is yet day
And we cannot go to sleep
Besides in the sky, the little birds fly
And the hills are all covered with sheep

Well well go & play till the light fades away
And then go home to bed
The little ones leaped & shouted & laugh'd
And all the hills ecchoed

## Infant Joy

I have no name
I am but two days old. –
What shall I call thee?
I happy am
Joy is my name, –
Sweet joy befall thee!

Pretty joy!
Sweet joy but two days old.
Sweet joy I call thee:
Thou dost smile.
I sing the while
Sweet joy befall thee.

# A Dream

Once a dream did weave a shade,
O'er my Angel-guarded bed,
That an Emmet lost it's way
Where on grass methought I lay.

Troubled wilderd and folorn
Dark benighted travel-worn,
Over many a tangled spray
All heart-broke I heard her say.

O my children! do they cry
Do they hear their father sigh.
Now they look abroad to see,
Now return and weep for me.

Pitying I drop'd a tear:
But I saw a glow-worm near:
Who replied. What wailing wight
Calls the watchman of the night.

I am set to light the ground,
While the beetle goes his round:
Follow now the beetles hum,
Little wanderer hie thee home.

## On Anothers Sorrow

Can I see anothers woe,
And not be in sorrow too.
Can I see anothers grief,
And not seek for kind relief.

Can I see a falling tear,
And not feel my sorrows share,
Can a father see his child,
Weep, nor be with sorrow fill'd.

Can a mother sit and hear,
An infant groan an infant fear –
No no never can it be.
Never never can it be.

And can he who smiles on all
Hear the wren with sorrows small,
Hear the small birds grief & care
Hear the woes that infants bear –

And not sit beside the nest
Pouring pity in their breast,
And not sit the cradle near
Weeping tear on infants tear.

And not sit both night & day,
Wiping all our tears away.
O! no never can it be.
Never never can it be.

He doth give his joy to all.
He becomes an infant small.
He becomes a man of woe
He doth feel the sorrow too.

Think not, thou canst sigh a sigh,
And thy maker is not by.

Think not, thou canst weep a tear,
And thy maker is not near.

O! he gives to us his joy,
That our grief he may destroy
Till our grief is fled & gone
He doth sit by us and moan

# The Little Girl Lost

In futurity
I prophetic see,
That the earth from sleep,
(Grave the sentence deep)

Shall arise and seek
For her maker meek:
And the desart wild
Become a garden mild.

In the southern clime,
Where the summers prime,
Never fades away;
Lovely Lyca lay.

Seven summers old
Lovely Lyca told.
She had wanderd long,
Hearing wild birds song.

Sweet sleep come to me
Underneath this tree;
Do father, mother weep. –
'Where can Lyca sleep'.

Lost in desart wild
Is your little child.
How can Lyca sleep,
If her mother weep.

If her heart does ake,
Then let Lyca wake;
If my mother sleep,
Lyca shall not weep.

Frowning frowning night,
O'er this desart bright,
Let thy moon arise,
While I close my eyes.

Sleeping Lyca lay;
While the beasts of prey,
Come from caverns deep,
View'd the maid asleep

The kingly lion stood
And the virgin view'd,
Then he gambold round
O'er the hallowd ground:

Leopards, tygers play,
Round her as she lay;
While the lion old,
Bow'd his mane of gold.

And her bosom lick,
And upon her neck,
From his eyes of flame,
Ruby tears there came;

While the lioness,
Loos'd her slender dress,
And naked they convey'd
To caves the sleeping maid.

# The Little Girl Found

All the night in woe
Lyca's parents go:
Over vallies deep,
While the desarts weep.

Tired and woe-begone,
Hoarse with making moan:
Arm in arm seven days,
They trac'd the desart ways.

Seven nights they sleep,
Among shadows deep:
And dream they see their child
Starv'd in desert wild.

Pale thro pathless ways
The fancied image strays,
Famish'd, weeping, weak
With hollow piteous shriek

Rising from unrest,
The trembling woman prest,
With feet of weary woe;
She could no further go.

In his arms he bore,
Her arm'd with sorrow sore;
Till before their way,
A couching lion lay.

Turning back was vain,
Soon his heavy mane,
Bore them to the ground;
Then he stalk'd around,

Smelling to his prey.
But their fears allay,
When he licks their hands;
And silent by them stands.

They look upon his eyes
Fill'd with deep surprise:
And wondering behold,
A spirit arm'd in gold.

On his head a crown
On his shoulders down,
Flow'd his golden hair.
Gone was all their care.

Follow me he said,
Weep not for the maid;
In my palace deep,
Lyca lies asleep.

Then they followed,
Where the vision led:
And saw their sleeping child,
Among tygers wild.

To this day they dwell
In a lonely dell
Nor fear the wolvish howl,
Nor the lions growl.

## The School Boy

I love to rise in a summer morn,
When the birds sing on every tree;
The distant huntsman winds his horn,
And the sky-lark sings with me.
O! what sweet company.

But to go to school in a summer morn
O! it drives all joy away;
Under a cruel eye outworn,
The little ones spend the day,
In sighing and dismay.

Ah! then at times I drooping sit,
And spend many an anxious hour.
Nor in my book can I take delight,
Nor sit in learnings bower,
Worn thro' with the dreary shower

How can the bird that is born for joy,
Sit in a cage and sing.
How can a child when fears annoy,
But droop his tender wing,
And forget his youthful spring.

O! father & mother, if buds are nip'd,
And blossoms blown away,
And if the tender plants are strip'd
Of their joy in the springing day,
By sorrow and cares dismay,

How shall the summer arise in joy
Or the summer fruits appear
Or how shall we gather what griefs destroy
Or bless the mellowing year,
When the blasts of winter appear.

## The Voice of the Ancient Bard

Youth of delight come hither:
And see the opening morn,
Image of truth new born
Doubt is fled & clouds of reason
Dark disputes & artful teazing.
Folly is an endless maze,
Tangled roots perplex her ways,
How many have fallen there!
They stumble all night over bones of the dead;
And feel they know not what but care;
And wish to lead others when they should be led.

## Thel's Motto

Does the Eagle know what is in the pit?
Or wilt thou go ask the Mole:
Can Wisdom be put in a silver rod?
Or Love in a golden bowl?

### THE ARGUMENT

Rintrah roars & shakes his fires in the burdend air;
Hungry clouds swag on the deep

Once meek, and in a perilous path,
The just man kept his course along
The vale of death.
Roses are planted where thorns grow.
And on the barren heath
Sing the honey bees.

Then the perilous path was planted:
And a river, and a spring
On every cliff and tomb;
And on the bleached bones
Red clay brought forth.

Till the villain left the paths of ease,
To walk in perilous paths, and drive
The just man into barren climes.

Now the sneaking serpent walks
In mild humility.
And the just man rages in the wilds
Where lions roam.

Rintrah roars & shakes his fires in the burdend air;
Hungry clouds swag on the deep.


As a new heaven is begun, and it is now thirty-three years since
its advent: the Eternal Hell revives. And lo! Swedenborg is the
Angel sitting at the tomb; his writings are the linen clothes

folded up. Now is the dominion of Edom, & the return of Adam into Paradise; see Isaiah xxxiv & XXXV Chap:

Without Contraries is no progression. Attraction and Repulsion, Reason and Energy, Love and Hate, are necessary to Human existence.

From these contraries spring what the religious call Good & Evil. Good is the passive that obeys Reason[.] Evil is the active springing from Energy.

Good is Heaven. Evil is Hell.

### THE VOICE OF THE DEVIL

All Bibles or sacred codes have been the causes of the following Errors.

1. That Man has two real existing principles Viz: a Body & a Soul.

2. That Energy calld Evil is alone from the Body & that Reason calld Good is alone from the Soul.

3. That God will torment Man in Eternity for following his Energies.

But the following Contraries to these are True

1 Man has no Body distinct from his Soul for that calld Body is a portion of Soul discernd by the five Senses, the chief inlets of Soul in this age

2 Energy is the only life and is from the Body and Reason is the bound or outward circumference of Energy.

3 Energy is Eternal Delight

Those who restrain desire, do so because theirs is weak enough to be restrained; and the restrainer or reason usurps its place & governs the unwilling.

And being restrand it by degrees becomes passive till it is only the shadow of desire.

The history of this is written in Paradise Lost. & the Governor or Reason is call'd Messiah.

And the original Archangel or possessor of the command of the heavenly host, is called the Devil or Satan and his children are call'd Sin & Death

But in the Book of Job Miltons Messiah is call'd Satan.

For this history has been adopted by both parties

It indeed appear'd to Reason as if Desire was cast out, but the Devils account is, that the Messiah fell. & formed a heaven of what he stole from the Abyss

This is shewn in the Gospel, where he prays to the Father to send the comforter or Desire that Reason may have Ideas to build on, the Jehovah of the Bible being no other than he, who dwells in flaming fire. Know that after Christs death, he became Jehovah.

But in Milton; the Father is Destiny, the Son, a Ratio of the five senses. & the Holy-ghost, Vacuum!

Note. The reason Milton wrote in fetters when he wrote of Angels & God, and at liberty when of Devils & Hell, is because he was a true Poet and of the Devils party without knowing it

A MEMORABLE FANCY

As I was walking among the fires of hell, delighted with the enjoyments of Genius; which to Angels look like torment and insanity. I collected some of their Proverbs: thinking that as the sayings used in a nation, mark its character, so the Proverbs of Hell, shew the nature of Infernal wisdom better than any description of buildings or garments.

When I came home; on the abyss of the five senses, where a flat sided steep frowns over the present world. I saw a mighty

Devil folded in black clouds, hovering on the sides of the rock, with corroding fires he wrote the following sentence now percieved by the minds of men, & read by them on earth.

How do you know but ev'ry Bird that cuts the airy way, Is an immense world of delight, clos'd by your senses five?

PROVERBS OF HELL

In seed time learn, in harvest teach, in winter enjoy.
Drive your cart and your plow over the bones of the dead.
The road of excess leads to the palace of wisdom.
Prudence is a rich ugly old maid courted by Incapacity.
He who desires but acts not, breeds pestilence.
The cut worm forgives the plow.
Dip him in the river who loves water.
A fool sees not the same tree that a wise man sees.
He whose face gives no light, shall never become a star.
Eternity is in love with the productions of time.
The busy bee has no time for sorrow.
The hours of folly are measur'd by the clock, but of wisdom:
    no clock can measure.
All wholsom food is caught without a net or a trap.
Bring out number weight & measure in a year of dearth.
No bird soars too high if he soars with his own wings.
A dead body revenges not injuries.
The most sublime act is to set another before you.
If the fool would persist in his folly he would become wise
Folly is the cloke of knavery.
Shame is Prides cloke.

Prisons are built with stones of Law, Brothels with bricks of
    Religion.

The pride of the peacock is the glory of God.

The lust of the goat is the bounty of God.

The wrath of the lion is the wisdom of God.

The nakedness of woman is the work of God.

Excess of sorrow laughs. Excess of joy weeps.

The roaring of lions, the howling of wolves, the raging of the stormy sea, and the destructive sword are portions of eternity too great for the eye of man.

The fox condemns the trap, not himself.

Joys impregnate. Sorrows bring forth.

Let man wear the fell of the lion woman the fleece of the sheep.

The bird a nest, the spider a web, man friendship.

The selfish smiling fool. & the sullen frowning fool. shall be both thought wise that they may be a rod.

What is now proved was once, only imagin'd.

The rat, the mouse, the fox, the rabbet; watch the roots, the lion, the tyger, the horse, the elephant, watch the fruits.

The cistern contains: the fountain overflows

One thought fills immensity.

Always be ready to speak your mind, and a base man will avoid you.

Every thing possible to be believ'd is an image of truth.

The eagle never lost so much time as when he submitted to learn of the crow.


The fox provides for himself but God provides for the lion.

Think in the morning, Act in the noon, Eat in the evening, Sleep in the night.

He who has sufferd you to impose on him knows you.

As the plow follows words, so God rewards prayers.

The tygers of wrath are wiser than the horses of instruction

Expect poison from the standing water.

You never know what is enough unless you know what is more than enough.

Listen to the fools reproach! it is a kingly title!

The eyes of fire, the nostrils of air, the mouth of water, the beard of earth.

The weak in courage is strong in cunning.

The apple tree never asks the beech how he shall grow, nor the lion, the horse, how he shall take his prey.

The thankful reciever bears a plentiful harvest.

If others had not been foolish, we should be so.

The soul of sweet delight, can never be defil'd,

When thou seest an Eagle, thou seest a portion of Genius lift up thy head!

As the catterpiller chooses the fairest leaves to lay her eggs on, so the priest lays his curse on the fairest joys.

To create a little flower is the labour of ages.

Damn braces: Bless relaxes.

The best wine is the oldest the best water the newest.

Prayers plow not! Praises reap not!

Joys laugh not! Sorrows weep not!


The head Sublime, the heart Pathos, the genitals Beauty, the hands & feet Proportion.

As the air to a bird or the sea to a fish, so is contempt to the contemptible.

The crow wish'd every thing was black, the owl, that every thing was white.

Exuberance is Beauty.

If the lion was advis'd by the fox he would be cunning.

Improve[me]nt makes strait roads, but the crooked roads without Improvement, are roads of Genius.

Sooner murder an infant in its cradle than nurse unacted desires

Where man is not nature is barren.

Truth can never be told so as to be understood, and not be believ'd.

Enough! or Too much

The ancient Poets animated all sensible objects with Gods or Geniuses, calling them by the names and adorning them with the properties of woods, rivers, mountains, lakes, cities, nations, and whatever their enlarged & numerous senses could percieve.

And particularly they studied the genius of each city & country placing it under its mental deity.

Till a system was formed, which some took advantage of & enslav'd the vulgar by attempting to realize or abstract the mental deities from their objects; thus began Priesthood.

Choosing forms of worship from poetic tales.

And at length they pronounced that the Gods had ordered such things.

Thus men forgot that All deities reside in the human breast.

A MEMORABLE FANCY

The Prophets Isaiah and Ezekiel dined with me, and I asked them how they dared so roundly to assert that God spake to them; and whether they did not think at the time, that they would be misunderstood, & so be the cause of imposition.

Isaiah answer'd. I saw no God nor heard any, in a finite organical perception; but my senses discover'd the infinite in every thing, and as I was then perswaded, & remain confirm'd; that the voice of honest indignation is the voice of God, I cared not for consequences but wrote.

Then I asked: does a firm perswasion that a thing is so, make it so?

He replied. All poets believe that it does, & in ages of imagination this firm perswasion removed mountains; but many are not capable of a firm perswasion of any thing.

Then Ezekiel said. The philosophy of the east taught the first principles of human perception some nations held one principle for the origin & some another, we of Israel taught that the Poetic Genius (as you now call it) was the first principle and all the others merely derivative, which was the cause of our despising the Priests & Philosophers of other countries, and prophecying that all Gods would at last be proved to originate in ours & to be the tributaries of the Poetic Genius, it was this that our great poet King David desired so fervently & invokes so patheticly, saying by this he conquers enemies & governs kingdoms; and we so loved our God that we cursed in his name all the deities of surrounding nations, and asserted that they had rebelled; from these opinions the vulgar came to think that all nations would at last be subject to the jews.

This said he, like all firm perswasions, is come to pass, for all nations believe the jews code and worship the jews god, and what greater subjection can be

I heard this with some wonder, & must confess my own conviction. After dinner I ask'd Isaiah to favour the world with his lost works, he said none of equal value was lost. Ezekiel said the same of his.

I also asked Isaiah what made him go naked and barefoot three years? he answered, the same that made our friend Diogenes the Grecian.

I then asked Ezekiel why he eat dung, & lay so long on his right & left side? he answered the desire of raising other men into a perception of the infinite this the North American tribes practise & is he honest who resists his genius or conscience only for the sake of present ease or gratification?

The ancient tradition that the world will be consumed in fire at the end of six thousand years is true as I have heard from Hell.

For the cherub with his flaming sword is hereby commanded to leave his guard at tree of life, and when he does, the whole creation will be consumed, and appear infinite and holy whereas it now appears finite & corrupt.

This will come to pass by an Improvement of sensual enjoyment.

But first the notion that man has a body distinct from his soul, is to be expunged; this I shall do, by printing in the infernal method by corrosives, which in Hell are salutory and medicinal, melting apparent surfaces away, and displaying the infinite which was hid.

If the doors of perception were cleansed every thing would appear to man as it is, infinite.

For man has closed himself up, till he sees all things thro' narrow chinks of his cavern.

A MEMORABLE FANCY

I was in a Printing house in Hell & saw the method in which knowledge is transmitted from generation to generation.

In the first chamber was a Dragon-Man, clearing away the rubbish from a caves mouth; within, a number of Dragons were hollowing the cave,

In the second chamber was a Viper folding round the rock & the cave, and others adorning it with gold silver and precious stones.

In the third chamber was an Eagle with wings and feathers of air, he caused the inside of the cave to be infinite, around were numbers of Eagle like men, who built palaces in the immense cliffs.

In the fourth chamber were Lions of flaming fire raging around & melting the metals into living fluids.

In the fifth chamber were Unnam'd forms, which cast the metals into the expanse.

There they were reciev'd by Men who occupied the sixth chamber, and took the forms of books & were arranged in libraries.

The Giants who formed this world into its sensual existence and now seem to live in it in chains, are in truth the causes of its life & the sources of all activity, but the chains are, the cunning of weak and tame minds which have power to resist energy, according to the proverb, the weak in courage is strong in cunning.

Thus one portion of being, is the Prolific the other, the Devouring: to the devourer it seems as if the producer was in his chains, but it is not so, he only takes portions of existence and fancies that the whole.

But the Prolific would cease to be Prolific unless the Devourer as a sea recieved the excess of his delights.

Some will say, Is not God alone the Prolific? I answer, God only Acts & Is, in existing beings or Men.

These two classes of men are always upon earth, & they should be enemies; whoever tries to reconcile them seeks to destroy existence.

Religion is an endeavour to reconcile the two.

Note. Jesus Christ did not wish to unite but to separate them, as in the Parable of sheep and goats! & he says I came not to send Peace but a Sword.

Messiah or Satan or Tempter was formerly thought to be one of the Antediluvians who are our Energies.

A MEMORABLE FANCY

An Angel came to me and said O pitiable foolish young man! O horrible! O dreadful state! consider the hot burning dungeon thou art preparing for thyself to all eternity, to which thou art going in such career.

I said perhaps you will be willing to shew me my eternal lot & we will contemplate together upon it and see whether your lot or mine is most desirable

So he took me thro' a stable & thro' a church & down into the church vault at the end of which was a mill: thro' the mill we went, and came to a cave down the winding cavern we groped our tedious way till a void boundless as a nether sky appeard beneath us & we held by the roots of trees and hung over this immensity, but I said, if you please we will commit ourselves to this void, and see whether providence is here also, if you will not I will? but he answerd, do not presume O young-man but as we here remain behold thy lot which will soon appear when the darkness passes away.

So I remaind with him sitting in the twisted root of an oak. he was suspended in a fungus which hung with the head downward into the deep;

By degrees we beheld the infinite Abyss, fiery as the smoke of a burning city; beneath us at an immense distance was the sun, black but shining[;] round it were fiery tracks on which revolv'd vast spiders, crawling after their prey; which flew or rather swum in the infinite deep, in the most terrific shapes of animals sprung from corruption. & the air was full of them, & seemd composed of them; these are Devils and are called Powers of the air, I now asked my companion which was my eternal lot? he said, between the black & white spiders

But now, from between the black & white spiders a cloud and fire burst and rolled thro the deep blackning all beneath, so that the nether deep grew black as a sea & rolled with a terrible noise: beneath us was nothing now to be seen but a black tempest, till looking east between the clouds & the waves. we saw a cataract of blood mixed with fire and not many stones throw from us appeard and sunk again the scaly fold of a monstrous serpent[;] at last to the east, distant about three degrees appeard a fiery crest above the waves slowly it reared like a ridge of golden rocks till we discoverd two globes of crimson fire, from which the sea fled away in clouds of smoke, and now we saw, it was the head of Leviathan, his forehead was divided into streaks of green & purple like those on a tygers forehead: soon we saw his mouth & red gills hang just above the raging foam tinging the black deep with beams of blood, advancing toward us with all the fury of a spiritual existence.

My friend the Angel climb'd up from his station into the mill; I remain'd alone, & then this appearance was no more, but I found myself sitting on a pleasant bank beside a river by moon light hearing a harper who sung to the harp, & his theme was, The man who never alters his opinion is like standing water, & breeds reptiles of the mind.

But I arose, and sought for the mill, & there I found my Angel, who surprised asked me, how I escaped?

I answerd. All that we saw was owing to your metaphysics: for when you ran away, I found myself on a bank by moonlight hearing a harper, But now we have seen my eternal lot, shall I shew you yours? he laughd at my proposal; but I by force suddenly caught him in my arms, & flew westerly thro' the night, till we were elevated above the earths shadow: then I flung myself with him directly into the body of the sun, here I clothed myself in white, & taking in my hand Swedenborgs volumes sunk from the glorious clime, and passed all the planets till we came to saturn, here I staid to rest & then leap'd into the void between saturn & the fixed stars.

Here said I! is your lot, in this space, if space it may be calld, Soon we saw the stable and the church, & I took him to the altar and open'd the Bible, and lo! it was a deep pit, into which I descended driving the Angel before me, soon we saw seven houses of brick, one we enterd; in it were a number of monkeys, baboons, & all of that species chaind by the middle, grinning and snatching at one another, but witheld by the shortness of their chains: however I saw that they sometimes grew numerous, and then the weak were caught by the strong and with a grinning aspect, first coupled with & then devourd, by plucking off first one limb and then another till the body was left a helpless trunk this after grinning & kissing it with seeming fondness they devourd too; and here & there I saw one savourily picking the flesh off his own tail; as the stench terribly annoyd us both we went into the mill, & I in my hand brought the skeleton of a body, which in the mill was Aristotles Analytics.

So the Angel said: thy phantasy has imposed upon me & thou oughtest to be ashamed.

I answered: we impose on one another, & it is but lost time to converse with you whose works are only Analytics

Opposition is true Friendship.

I have always found that Angels have the vanity to speak of themselves as the only wise; this they do with a confident insolence sprouting from systematic reasoning:

Thus Swedenborg boasts that what he writes is new: tho' it is only the Contents or Index of already publish'd books

A man carried a monkey about for a shew. & because he was a little wiser than the monkey, grew vain and conciev'd himself as much wiser than seven men. It is so with Swedenborg; he shews the folly of churches & exposes hypocrites, till he imagines that all are religious. & himself the single one on earth that ever broke a net.

Now hear a plain fact: Swedenborg has not written one new truth: Now hear another: he has written all the old falshoods.

And now hear the reason. He conversed with Angels who are all religious, & conversed not with Devils who all hate religion, for he was incapable thro' his conceited notions.

Thus Swedenborgs writings are a recapitulation of all superficial opinions, and an analysis of the more sublime but no further.

Have now another plain fact: Any man of mechanical talents may from the writings of Paracelsus or Jacob Behmen, produce ten thousand volumes of equal value with Swedenborg's and from those of Dante or Shakespear, an infinite number.

But when he has done this, let him not say that he knows better than his master, for he only holds a candle in sunshine.

A MEMORABLE FANCY

Once I saw a Devil in a flame of fire who arose before an Angel that sat on a cloud and the Devil utterd these words.

The worship of God is. Honouring his gifts in other men each according to his genius and loving the greatest men best, those who envy or calumniate great men hate God, for there is no other God.

The Angel hearing this became almost blue but mastering himself he grew yellow, & at last white pink & smiling and then replied,

Thou Idolater, is not God One? & is not he visible in Jesus Christ? and has not Jesus Christ given his sanction to the law of ten commandments and are not all other men fools, sinners, & nothings?

The Devil answer'd; bray a fool in a morter with wheat yet shall not his folly be beaten out of him: if Jesus Christ is the greatest man, you ought to love him in the greatest degree; now hear how he has given his sanction to the law of ten commandments: did he not mock at the sabbath, and so mock the sabbaths God? murder those who were murderd because of him? turn away the law from the woman taken in adultery? steal the labor of others to support him? bear false witness when he omitted making a defence before Pilate? covet when he pray'd for his disciples, and when he bid them shake off the dust of their feet against such as refused to lodge them? I tell you, no virtue can exist without breaking these ten commandments ∴ Jesus was all virtue, and acted from impulse not from rules.

When he had so spoken: I beheld the Angel who stretched out his arms embracing the flame of fire & he was consumed and arose as Elijah.

Note. This Angel, who is now become a Devil, is my particular friend: we often read the Bible together in its infernal or diabolical sense which the world shall have if they behave well

I have also: The Bible of Hell: which the world shall have whether they will or no.

One Law for the Lion & Ox is Oppression

A SONG OF LIBERTY

1. The Eternal Female groand! it was heard over all the Earth:

2. Albions coast is sick silent; the American meadows faint!

3. Shadows of Prophecy shiver along by the lakes and the rivers and mutter across the ocean? France rend down thy dungeon;

4. Golden Spain burst the barriers of old Rome;

5. Cast thy keys O Rome into the deep down falling, even to eternity down falling,

6. And weep

7. In her trembling hands she took the new born terror howling:

8. On those infinite mountains of light now barr'd out by the atlantic sea, the new born fire stood before the starry king!

9. Flag'd with grey brow'd snows and thunderous visages the jealous wings wav'd over the deep.

10. The speary hand burned aloft, unbuckled was the shield, forth went the hand of jealousy among the flaming hair, and hurl'd the new born wonder thro' the starry night.

11. The fire, the fire, is falling!

12. Look up! look up! O citizen of London enlarge thy countenance; O Jew, leave counting gold! return to thy oil

and wine; O African! black African! (go. winged thought widen his forehead.)

13. The fiery limbs, the flaming hair, shot like the sinking sun into the western sea.

14. Wak'd from his eternal sleep, the hoary element roaring fled away:

15. Down rushd beating his wings in vain the jealous king; his grey brow'd councellors, thunderous warriors, curl'd veterans, among helms, and shields, and chariots[,] horses, elephants: banners, castles, slings and rocks,

16. Falling, rushing, ruining! buried in the ruins, on Urthona's dens.

17. All night beneath the ruins, then their sullen flames faded emerge round the gloomy king,

18. With thunder and fire: leading his starry hosts thro' the waste wilderness he promulgates his ten commands, glancing his beamy eyelids over the deep in dark dismay,

19. Where the son of fire in his eastern cloud, while the morning plumes her golden breast.

20. Spurning the clouds written with curses stamps the stony law to dust, loosing the eternal horses from the dens of night, crying

Empire is no more! and now the lion & wolf shall cease.

CHORUS

Let the Priests of the Raven of dawn, no longer in deadly black with hoarse note curse the sons of joy. Nor his accepted brethren whom, tyrant, he calls free: lay the bound or build the roof. Nor pale religious letchery call that virginity, that wishes but acts not!

For every thing that lives is Holy

## Introduction

Hear the voice of the Bard!
Who Present, Past, & Future sees
Whose ears have heard,
The Holy Word,
That walk'd among the ancient trees.

Calling the lapsed Soul
And weeping in the evening dew:
That might controll,
The starry pole;
And fallen fallen light renew!

O Earth O Earth return!
Arise from out the dewy grass;
Night is worn,
And the morn
Rises from the slumberous mass.

Turn away no more:
Why wilt thou turn away
The starry floor
The watry shore
Is giv'n thee till the break of day.

# Earth's Answer

Earth rais'd up her head,
From the darkness dread & drear.
Her light fled:
Stony dread!
And her locks cover'd with grey despair.

Prison'd on watry shore
Starry Jealousy does keep my den
Cold and hoar
Weeping o'er
I hear the Father of the ancient men

Selfish father of men
Cruel jealous selfish fear
Can delight
Chain'd in night
The virgins of youth and morning bear.

Does spring hide its joy
When buds and blossoms grow?
Does the sower?
Sow by night?
Or the plowman in darkness plow?

Break this heavy chain,
That does freeze my bones around
Selfish! vain,
Eternal bane!
That free Love with bondage bound.

# The Clod & the Pebble

Love seeketh not Itself to please,
Nor for itself hath any care;
But for another gives its ease,
And builds a Heaven in Hells despair.

    So sang a little Clod of Clay,
    Trodden with the cattles feet:
    But a Pebble of the brook,
    Warbled out these metres meet.

Love seeketh only Self to please,
To bind another to its delight;
Joys in anothers loss of ease,
And builds a Hell in Heavens despite.

## Holy Thursday

Is this a holy thing to see,
In a rich and fruitful land,
Babes reduced to misery,
Fed with cold and usurous hand?

Is that trembling cry a song?
Can it be a song of joy?
And so many children poor?
It is a land of poverty!

And their sun does never shine.
And their fields are bleak & bare.
And their ways are fill'd with thorns.
It is eternal winter there.

For where-e'er the sun does shine,
And where-e'er the rain does fall:
Babe can never hunger there,
Nor poverty the mind appall.

.

## The Chimney Sweeper

A little black thing among the snow:
Crying weep, weep in notes of woe!
Where are thy father & mother? say?
They are both gone up to the church to pray.

Because I was happy upon the heath.
And smil'd among the winters snow:
They clothed me in the clothes of death.
And taught me to sing the notes of woe.

And because I am happy & dance & sing.
They think they have done me no injury:
And are gone to praise God & his Priest & King
Who make up a heaven of our misery.

## Nurses Song

When the voices of children, are heard on the green
And whisperings are in the dale:
The days of my youth rise fresh in my mind,
My face turns green and pale.

Then come home my children, the sun is gone down
And the dews of night arise
Your spring & your day, are wasted in play
And your winter and night in disguise.

## The Sick Rose

O Rose thou art sick.
The invisible worm,
That flies in the night
In the howling storm:

Has found out thy bed
Of crimson joy:
And his dark secret love
Does thy life destroy.

## The Fly

Little Fly
Thy summers play,
My thoughtless hand
Has brush'd away.

Am not I
A fly like thee?
Or art not thou
A man like me?

For I dance
And drink & sing;
Till some blind hand
Shall brush my wing.

If thought is life
And strength & breath;
And the want
Of thought is death;

Then am I
A happy fly,
If I live,
Or if I die.

## The Angel

I Dreamt a Dream! what can it mean?
And that I was a maiden Queen:
Guarded by an Angel mild;
Witless woe, was ne'er beguil'd!

And I wept both night and day
And he wip'd my tears away
And I wept both day and night
And hid from him my hearts delight

So he took his wings and fled:
Then the morn blush'd rosy red:
I dried my tears & armd my fears,
With ten thousand shields and spears.

Soon my Angel came again:
I was arm'd, he came in vain:
For the time of youth was fled
And grey hairs were on my head.

## The Tyger

Tyger Tyger, burning bright,
In the forests of the night:
What immortal hand or eye,
Could frame thy fearful symmetry?

In what distant deeps or skies
Burnt the fire of thine eyes!
On what wings dare he aspire?
What the hand, dare sieze the fire?

And what shoulder, & what art,
Could twist the sinews of thy heart?
And when thy heart began to beat,
What dread hand? & what dread feet?

What the hammer? what the chain,
In what furnace was thy brain?
What the anvil? what dread grasp,
Dare its deadly terrors clasp?

When the stars threw down their spears
And water'd heaven with their tears:
Did he smile his work to see?
Did he who made the Lamb make thee?

Tyger, Tyger burning bright,
In the forests of the night:
What immortal hand or eye,
Dare frame thy fearful symmetry?

## My Pretty Rose Tree

A flower was offerd to me;
Such a flower as May never bore.
But I said I've a Pretty Rose-tree.
And I passed the sweet flower o'er.

Then I went to my Pretty Rose-tree;
To tend her by day and by night.
But my Rose turned away with jealousy:
And her thorns were my only delight.

# Ah! Sun-Flower

Ah Sun-flower! weary of time.
Who countest the steps of the Sun:
Seeking after that sweet golden clime
Where the travellers journey is done.

Where the Youth pined away with desire,
And the pale Virgin shrouded in snow:
Arise from their graves and aspire,
Where my Sun-flower wishes to go.

## The Lilly

The modest Rose puts forth a thorn:
The humble Sheep, a threatning horn:
While the Lilly white, shall in Love delight,
Nor a thorn nor a threat stain her beauty bright

## The Garden of Love

I went to the Garden of Love.
And saw what I never had seen:
A Chapel was built in the midst,
Where I used to play on the green.

And the gates of this Chapel were shut,
And Thou shalt not. writ over the door;
So I turn'd to the Garden of Love,
That so many sweet flowers bore.

And I saw it was filled with graves,
And tomb-stones where flowers should be:
And Priests in black gowns, were walking their rounds,
And binding with briars, my joys & desires.

# The Little Vagabond

Dear Mother, dear Mother, the Church is cold.
But the Ale-house is healthy & pleasant & warm;
Besides I can tell where I am use'd well,
Such usage in heaven will never do well.

But if at the Church they would give us some Ale.
And a pleasant fire, our souls to regale;
We'd sing and we'd pray, all the live-long day;
Nor ever once wish from the Church to stray,

Then the Parson might preach & drink & sing.
And we'd be as happy as birds in the spring:
And modest dame Lurch, who is always at Church,
Wou'ld not have bandy children nor fasting nor birch.

And God like a father rejoicing to see,
His children as pleasant and happy as he:
Would have no more quarrel with the Devil or the Barrel
But kiss him & give him both drink and apparel.

## London

I wander thro' each charter'd street,
Near where the charter'd Thames does flow.
And mark in every face I meet
Marks of weakness, marks of woe.

In every cry of every Man,
In every Infants cry of fear,
In every voice: in every ban,
The mind-forg'd manacles I hear

How the Chimney-sweepers cry
Every blackning Church appalls,
And the hapless Soldiers sigh,
Runs in blood down Palace walls

But most thro' midnight streets I hear
How the youthful Harlots curse
Blasts the new-born Infants tear
And blights with plagues the Marriage hearse

## The Human Abstract

Pity would be no more,
If we did not make somebody Poor:
And Mercy no more could be,
If all were as happy as we;

And mutual fear brings peace;
Till the selfish loves increase.
Then Cruelty knits a snare,
And spreads his baits with care.

He sits down with holy fears,
And waters the ground with tears:
Then Humility takes its root
Underneath his foot.

Soon spreads the dismal shade
Of Mystery over his head;
And the Catterpiller and Fly,
Feed on the Mystery.

And it bears the fruit of Deceit,
Ruddy and sweet to eat;
And the Raven his nest has made
In its thickest shade.

The Gods of the earth and sea,
Sought thro' Nature to find this Tree
But their search was all in vain:
There grows one in the Human Brain

## Infant Sorrow

My mother groand! my father wept.
Into the dangerous world I leapt:
Helpless, naked, piping loud;
Like a fiend hid in a cloud.

Struggling in my fathers hands:
Striving against my swadling bands:
Bound and weary I thought best
To sulk upon my mothers breast.

# A Poison Tree

I was angry with my friend:
I told my wrath, my wrath did end.
I was angry with my foe:
I told it not, my wrath did grow.

And I watered it in fears.
Night & morning with my tears:
And I sunned it with smiles.
And with soft deceitful wiles.

And it grew both day and night.
Till it bore an apple bright.
And my foe beheld it shine.
And he knew that it was mine.

And into my garden stole.
When the night had veild the pole;
In the morning glad I see;
My foe outstretchd beneath the tree.

# A Little Boy Lost

Nought loves another as itself
Nor venerates another so.
Nor is it possible to Thought
A greater than itself to know:

And Father, how can I love you,
Or any of my brothers more?
I love you like the little bird
That picks up crumbs around the door.

The Priest sat by and heard the child.
In trembling zeal he siez'd his hair:
He led him by his little coat:
And all admir'd the Priestly care.

And standing on the altar high,
Lo what a fiend is here! said he:
One who sets reason up for judge
Of our most holy Mystery.

The weeping child could not be heard.
The weeping parents wept in vain:
They strip'd him to his little shirt.
And bound him in an iron chain.

And burn'd him in a holy place,
Where many had been burn'd before:
The weeping parents wept in vain.
Are such things done on Albions shore.

# A Little Girl Lost

*Children of the future Age,*
*Reading this indignant page:*
*Know that in a former time,*
*Love! sweet Love! was thought a crime.*

In the Age of Gold,
Free from winters cold:
Youth and maiden bright,
To the holy light,
Naked in the sunny beams delight.

Once a youthful pair
Fill'd with softest care:
Met in garden bright,
Where the holy light,
Had just remov'd the curtains of the night.

There in rising day,
On the grass they play:
Parents were afar:
Strangers came not near:
And the maiden soon forgot her fear.

Tired with kisses sweet
They agree to meet,
When the silent sleep
Waves o'er heavens deep;
And the weary tired wanderers weep.

To her father white
Came the maiden bright:
But his loving look.
Like the holy book,
All her tender limbs with terror shook.

Ona! pale and weak!
To thy father speak:
O the trembling fear!
O the dismal care!
That shakes the blossoms of my hoary hair

## To Tirzah

Whate'er is Born of Mortal Birth,
Must be consumed with the Earth
To rise from Generation free;
Then what have I to do with thee?

The Sexes sprung from Shame & Pride
Blow'd in the morn: in evening died
But Mercy changd Death into Sleep;
The Sexes rose to work & weep.

Thou Mother of my Mortal part
With cruelty didst mould my Heart,
And with false self-decieving tears,
Didst bind my Nostrils Eyes & Ears.

Didst close my Tongue in senseless clay
And me to Mortal Life betray:
The Death of Jesus set me free,
Then what have I to do with thee?

# A Divine Image

   Cruelty has a Human Heart
And Jealousy a Human Face
Terror the Human Form Divine
And Secrecy the Human Dress

The Human Dress is forged Iron
The Human Form a fiery Forge,
The Human Face a Furnace seal'd
The Human Heart its hungry Gorge.

*from* MILTON (1804–?8)

And did those feet in ancient time.
Walk upon Englands mountains green:
And was the holy Lamb of God,
On Englands pleasant pastures seen!

And did the Countenance Divine,
Shine forth upon our clouded hills?
And was Jerusalem builded here,
Among these dark Satanic Mills?

Bring me my Bow of burning gold:
Bring me my Arrows of desire:
Bring me my Spear: O clouds unfold!
Bring me my Chariot of fire!

I will not cease from Mental Fight,
Nor shall my Sword sleep in my hand:
Till we have built Jerusalem,
In Englands green & pleasant Land.


Would to God that all the Lords people were Prophets.
Numbers XI. ch 29 v.

*from* FOR THE SEXES (?1818)

## What is Man!

The Suns Light when he unfolds it
Depends on the Organ that beholds it

## The Gates of Paradise

Mutual forgiveness of each Vice
Such are the Gates of Paradise
Against the Accusers chief desire
Who walked among the Stones of Fire
Jehovahs Finger Wrote the Law
Then Wept! then rose in Zeal & Awe
And the Dead Corpse from Sinais heat
Buried beneath his Mercy Seat
O Christians Christians tell me Why
You rear it on your Altars high

## To the Accuser who is The God of this World

Truly My Satan thou art but a Dunce
And dost not know the Garment from the Man
Every Harlot was a Virgin once
Nor canst thou ever change Kate into Nan

Tho thou art Worshipd by the Names Divine
Of Jesus & Jehovah: thou art still
The Son of Morn in weary Nights decline
The lost Travellers Dream under the Hill

∾

Mock on Mock on Voltaire Rousseau
Mock on Mock on tis all in vain
You throw the sand against the wind
And the wind blows it back again

And every sand becomes a Gem
Reflected in the beams divine
Blown back they blind the mocking Eye
But still in Israels paths they shine

The Atoms of Democritus
And Newtons Particles of light
Are sands upon the Red sea shore
Where Israels tents do shine so bright

∾

A Petty sneaking Knave I knew
O M<sup>r</sup> Cr[omek] how do ye do

## Several Questions Answerd

He who binds to himself a joy
Doth the winged life destroy
But he who kisses the joy as it flies
Lives in Eternitys sun rise

The look of love alarms
Because tis filld with fire
But the look of soft deceit
Shall Win the lovers hire

Soft deceit & Idleness
These are Beautys sweetest dress

# The Question Answerd

What is it men [*of*] in women do require?
The lineaments of Gratified Desire.
What is it women do [*of*] in men require?
The lineaments of Gratified Desire.

# An Answer to the Parson

Why of the sheep do you not learn peace
Because I dont want you to shear my fleece

## The Smile

There is a Smile of Love
And there is a Smile of Deceit
And there is a Smile of Smiles
In which these two Smiles meet

And there is a Frown of Hate
And there is a Frown of disdain
And there is a Frown of Frowns
Which you strive to forget in vain

For it sticks in the Hearts deep Core
And it sticks in the deep Back bone
And no Smile that ever was smild
But only one Smile alone

That betwixt the Cradle & Grave
It only once Smild can be
But when it once is Smild
Theres an end to all Misery

# The Golden Net

Three Virgins at the break of day
Whither young Man whither away
Alas for woe! alas for woe!
They cry & tears for ever flow
The one was Clothd in flames of fire
The other Clothd in iron wire
The other Clothd in tears & sighs
Dazling bright before my Eyes
They bore a Net of Golden twine
To hang upon the Branches fine
Pitying I wept to see the woe
That Love & Beauty undergo
To be consumd in burning Fires
And in ungratified desires
And in tears clothd Night & day
Melted all my Soul away
When they saw my Tears a Smile
That did Heaven itself beguile
Bore the Golden Net aloft
As on downy Pinions soft
Over the Morning of my day
Underneath the Net I stray
Now intreating Burning Fire
Now intreating Iron Wire
Now intreating Tears & Sighs
O when will the morning rise

# The Mental Traveller

I traveld thro' a Land of Men
A Land of Men & Women too
And heard & saw such dreadful things
As cold Earth wanderers never knew

For there the Babe is born in joy
That was begotten in dire woe
Just as we Reap in joy the fruit
Which we in bitter tears did sow

And if the Babe is born a Boy
He's given to a Woman Old
Who nails him down upon a rock
Catches his shrieks in cups of gold

She binds iron thorns around his head
She pierces both his hands & feet
She cuts his heart out at his side
To make it feel both cold & heat

Her fingers number every Nerve
Just as a Miser counts his gold
She lives upon his shrieks & cries
And she grows young as he grows old

Till he becomes a bleeding youth
And she becomes a Virgin bright
Then he rends up his Manacles
And binds her down for his delight

He plants himself in all her Nerves
Just as a Husbandman his mould
And she becomes his dwelling place
And Garden fruitful seventy fold

An aged Shadow soon he fades
Wandring round in Earthly Cot
Full filled all with gems & gold
Which he by industry had got

And these are the gems of the Human Soul
The rubies & pearls of a lovesick eye
The countless gold of the akeing heart
The martyrs groan & the lovers sigh

They are his meat they are his drink
He feeds the Beggar & the Poor
And the wayfaring Traveller
For ever open is his door

His grief is their eternal joy
They make the roofs & walls to ring
Till from the fire on the hearth
A little Female Babe does spring

And she is all of solid fire
And gems & gold that none his hand
Dares stretch to touch her Baby form
Or wrap her in his swaddling-band

But She comes to the Man she loves
If young or old or rich or poor
They soon drive out the aged Host
A Beggar at anothers door

He wanders weeping far away
Untill some other take him in
Oft blind & age-bent sore distrest
Until he can a Maiden win

And to allay his freezing Age
The Poor Man takes her in his arms
The Cottage fades before his sight
The Garden & its lovely Charms

The Guests are scatterd thro' the land
For the Eye altering alters all
The Senses roll themselves in fear
And the flat Earth becomes a Ball

The Stars Sun Moon all shrink away
A desert vast without a bound
And nothing left to eat or drink
And a dark desert all around

The honey of her Infant lips
The bread & wine of her sweet smile
The wild game of her roving Eye
Does him to Infancy beguile

For as he eats & drinks he grows
Younger & younger every day
And on the desert wild they both
Wander in terror & dismay

Like the wild Stag she flees away
Her fear plants many a thicket wild
While he pursues her night & day
By various arts of Love beguild

By various arts of Love & Hate
Till the wide desert planted oer
With Labyrinths of wayward Love
Where roams the Lion Wolf & Boar

Till he becomes a wayward Babe
And she a weeping Woman Old
Then many a Lover wanders here
The Sun & Stars are nearer rolld

The trees bring forth sweet Extacy
To all who in the desert roam
Till many a City there is Built
And many a pleasant Shepherds home

But when they find the frowning Babe
Terror strikes thro the region wide
They cry the Babe the Babe is Born
And flee away on Every side

For who dare touch the frowning form
His arm is witherd to its root
Lions Boars Wolves all howling flee
And every Tree does shed its fruit

And none can touch that frowning form
Except it be a Woman Old
She nails him down upon the Rock
And all is done as I have told

# The Crystal Cabinet

The Maiden caught me in the Wild
Where I was dancing merrily
She put me into her Cabinet
And Lockd me up with a golden Key

This Cabinet is formd of Gold
And Pearl & Crystal shining bright
And within it opens into a World
And a little lovely Moony Night

Another England there I saw
Another London with its Tower
Another Thames & other Hills
And another pleasant Surrey Bower

Another Maiden like herself
Translucent lovely shining clear
Threefold each in the other closd
O what a pleasant trembling fear

O what a smile a threefold Smile
Filld me that like a flame I burnd
I bent to Kiss the lovely Maid
And found a Threefold Kiss returnd

I strove to sieze the inmost Form
With ardor fierce & hands of flame
But burst the Crystal Cabinet
And like a Weeping Babe became

A weeping Babe upon the wild
And Weeping Woman pale reclind
And in the outward air again
I filld with woes the passing Wind

# Auguries of Innocence

To see a World in a Grain of Sand
And a Heaven in a Wild Flower
Hold Infinity in the palm of your hand
And Eternity in an hour
A Robin Red breast in a Cage
Puts all Heaven in a Rage
A dove house filld with doves & Pigeons
Shudders Hell thro all its regions
A dog starvd at his Masters Gate
Predicts the ruin of the State
A Horse misusd upon the Road
Calls to Heaven for Human blood
Each outcry of the hunted Hare
A fibre from the Brain does tear
A Skylark wounded in the wing
A Cherubim does cease to sing
The Game Cock clipd & armd for fight
Does the Rising Sun affright
Every Wolfs & Lions howl
Raises from Hell a Human Soul
The wild deer wandring here & there
Keeps the Human Soul from Care
The Lamb misusd breeds Public strife
And yet forgives the Butchers Knife
The Bat that flits at close of Eve
Has left the Brain that wont Believe
The Owl that calls upon the Night
Speaks the Unbelievers fright
He who shall hurt the little Wren
Shall never be belovd by Men
He who the Ox to wrath has movd
Shall never be by Woman lovd
The wanton Boy that kills the Fly

Shall feel the Spiders enmity
He who torments the Chafers sprite
Weaves a Bower in endless Night
The Catterpiller on the Leaf
Repeats to thee thy Mothers grief
Kill not the Moth nor Butterfly
For the Last Judgment draweth nigh
He who shall train the Horse to War
Shall never pass the Polar Bar
The Beggers Dog & Widows Cat
Feed them & thou wilt grow fat
The Gnat that sings his Summers song
Poison gets from Slanders tongue
The poison of the Snake & Newt
Is the sweat of Envys Foot
The Poison of the Honey Bee
Is the Artists Jealousy
The Princes Robes & Beggars Rags
Are Toadstools on the Misers Bags
A truth thats told with bad intent
Beats all the Lies you can invent
It is right it should be so
Man was made for Joy & Woe
And when this we rightly know
Thro the World we safely go
Joy & Woe are woven fine
A Clothing for the Soul divine
Under every grief & pine
Runs a joy with silken twine
The Babe is more than swadling Bands
Throughout all these Human Lands
Tools were made & Born were hands
Every Farmer Understands
Every Tear from Every Eye
Becomes a Babe in Eternity
This is caught by Females bright

And returnd to its own delight
The Bleat the Bark Bellow & Roar
Are Waves that Beat on Heavens Shore
The Babe that weeps the Rod beneath
Writes Revenge in realms of death
The Beggars Rags fluttering in Air
Does to Rags the Heavens tear
The Soldier armd with Sword & Gun
Palsied strikes the Summers Sun
The poor Mans Farthing is worth more
Than all the Gold on Africs Shore
One Mite wrung from the Labrers hands
Shall buy & sell the Misers Lands
Or if protected from on high
Does that whole Nation sell & buy
He who mocks the Infants Faith
Shall be mock'd in Age & Death
He who shall teach the Child to Doubt
The rotting Grave shall neer get out
He who respects the Infants faith
Triumphs over Hell & Death
The Childs Toys & the Old Mans Reasons
Are the Fruits of the Two seasons
The Questioner who sits so sly
Shall never know how to Reply
He who replies to words of Doubt
Doth put the Light of Knowledge out
The Strongest Poison ever known
Came from Caesars Laurel Crown
Nought can deform the Human Race
Like to the Armours iron brace
When Gold & Gems adorn the Plow
To peaceful Arts shall Envy Bow
A Riddle or the Crickets Cry
Is to Doubt a fit Reply
The Emmets Inch & Eagles Mile

Make Lame Philosophy to smile
He who Doubts from what he sees
Will neer Believe do what you Please
If the Sun & Moon should doubt
Theyd immediately Go out
To be in a Passion you Good may do
But no Good if a Passion is in you
The Whore & Gambler by the State
Licencd build that Nations Fate
The Harlots cry from Street to Street
Shall weave Old Englands winding Sheet
The Winners Shout the Losers Curse
Dance before dead Englands Hearse
Every Night & every Morn
Some to Misery are Born
Every Morn & every Night
Some are Born to sweet delight
Some are Born to sweet delight
Some are Born to Endless Night
We are led to Believe a Lie
When we see [*with*] not Thro the Eye
Which was Born in a Night to perish in a Night
When the Soul Slept in Beams of Light
God Appears & God is Light
To those poor Souls who dwell in Night
But does a Human Form Display
To those who Dwell in Realms of day

# William Bond

I wonder whether the Girls are mad
And I wonder whether they mean to kill
And I wonder if William Bond will die
For assuredly he is very ill

He went to Church in a May morning
Attended by Fairies one two & three
But the Angels of Providence drove them away
And he returnd home in Misery

He went not out to the Field nor Fold
He went not out to the Village nor Town
But he came home in a black black cloud
And took to his Bed & there lay down

And an Angel of Providence at his Feet
And an Angel of Providence at his Head
And in the midst a Black Black Cloud
And in the midst the Sick Man on his Bed

And on his Right hand was Mary Green
And on his Left hand was his Sister Jane
And their tears fell thro the black black Cloud
To drive away the sick mans pain

O William if thou dost another Love
Dost another Love better than poor Mary
Go & take that other to be thy Wife
And Mary Green shall her Servant be

Yes Mary I do another Love
Another I Love far better than thee
And Another I will have for my Wife
Then what have I to do with thee

For thou art Melancholy Pale
And on thy Head is the cold Moons shine
But she is ruddy & bright as day
And the sun beams dazzle from her eyne

Mary trembled & Mary childd
And Mary fell down on the right hand floor
That William Bond & his Sister Jane
Scarce could recover Mary more

When Mary woke & found her Laid
On the Right hand of her William dear
On the Right hand of his loved Bed
And saw her William Bond so near

The Fairies that fled from William Bond
Danced around her Shining Head
They danced over the Pillow white
And the Angels of Providence left the Bed

I thought Love livd in the hot sun shine
But O he lives in the Moony light
I thought to find Love in the heat of day
But sweet Love is the Comforter of Night

Seek Love in the Pity of others Woe
In the gentle relief of anothers care
In the darkness of night & the winters snow
In the naked & outcast Seek Love there